The Dignity of Older People

and their Mission in the Church and in the World

PONTIFICAL COUNCIL FOR THE LAITY

*All CTS booklets
are published thanks to the
generous support of its Members*

CATHOLIC TRUTH SOCIETY
PUBLISHERS TO THE HOLY SEE

Published by the Catholic Truth Society with
the Catholic Media Office 1999

Text © Pontifical Council for the Laity

ISBN 1 86082 071 9

Front cover: Lakeside Landscape, Oil on Canvas,
Renoir, Pierre-Auguste, courtesy of the Trustees, the
National Gallery, London

Catholic Truth Society
40-46 Harleyford Road   London SE11 5AY
Tel: 0171 640 0042   Fax: 0171 640 0046

CONTENTS

INTRODUCTION

Scientific advances and the consequent progress of medicine have made a decisive contribution in recent decades to prolonging the average duration of human life. The term "third age" now embraces a large segment of the world's population: people who have retired from active employment, yet who still have great inner resources and are still able to contribute to the common good. To this huge throng of "young old" (as they are called by the new categories of old age defined by demographers, i.e. those aged between 65 and 70) is added a so-called fourth age, that of the "oldest old" (those over 75), whose ranks are likewise destined to become ever more numerous.[1]

The prolongation of average life expectancy, and the sometimes dramatic decrease in the birth rate, have given rise to an unprecedented demographic transition: the age pyramid that existed less than half a century ago has literally been turned upside down. The number of older people is constantly increasing, while that of the

1 The "population" section of the United Nations' Department of Economic and Social Affairs published new demographic estimates and projections on 26 October 1998. The chapter devoted to the growth in the number of older people suggests, *inter alia*, that the 66 million octogenarians and over 80 year-olds in the world today are destined to increase to 370 million in 2050, including an estimated 2·2 million centenarians.

respected, and hopes that the question may be tackled with a great sense of responsibility by everyone: by individuals, families, associations, governments and international organisations, each according to its own competencies and duties and in conformity with the very important principle of subsidiarity. Only in this way can older people be enabled to enjoy ever more human living conditions and play their indispensable role in a society undergoing a rapid and continuous process of economic and cultural change. Only in this way, moreover, can concerted action be taken to exert influence on the social, economic and educational systems in such a way as to provide all citizens, without discrimination, with the necessary resources to satisfy old and new needs, to ensure the effective protection of rights, and to restore grounds for trust and hope and a sense of belonging to all those excluded from active participation in the human community.

The Church's attention and commitment to older people are nothing new. She has directed her mission and pastoral care to older people in the most varied circumstances over the centuries. Christian *"caritas"* has embraced their needs; it has given rise to the most varied forms of apostolate at the service of older people, especially thanks to the initiative and concern of religious congregations and lay associations. The Church's teaching, far from considering the question as a mere problem of assistance and charity, has always reaffirmed the primary importance of recognising and fostering the intrinsic value of persons of all ages. She has continued to remind everyone of the need to ensure that the human and spiritual riches, the reserves of experience and wisdom accumulated in the course of entire lives, be not lost. In confirmation of this, Pope John Paul II, addressing about 8,000 older people received in audience on 23 March 1984, said: "Do not be surprised by the temptation of interior solitude. Notwithstanding the complexity of your problems, ... and the forces which gradually wear you down, and despite the inadequacies of social organisations, the delays of official legislation and a selfish society's failure to understand, you are not and must not consider yourselves to be on the margins of the life of the Church, passive elements in a world in excessive motion, but active subjects of a period in human existence which is rich in spirituality and humanity. You still have a mission to fulfil and a contribution to make".[4]

However, it has to be recognised that the current situation is unprecedented in many respects. It urges the Church to revise her approach to the pastoral care of older people in the third and fourth ages. New forms and methods, more consonant with the needs and

4 *Insegnamenti di Giovanni Paolo II*, VII, 1 (1984), p. 744.

spiritual aspirations of older people, need to be sought; new pastoral plans rooted in the defence of life, of its meaning and destiny, need to be formulated. These are essential conditions for encouraging older people to make their own contribution to the mission of the Church and helping them to derive particular spiritual enrichment from their active participation in the life of the ecclesial community.

This, broadly speaking, is the context in which the present document of the Pontifical Council for the Laity is placed. It was drawn up with the contribution of a working group consisting of representatives of the Holy See's Secretariat of State and various offices of the Roman Curia, as well as exponents of various ecclesial organisations (movements, associations, religious congregations) with lengthy experience in the world of older people. By placing this document at the disposal of Episcopal Conferences, bishops and priests, men and women religious, lay movements and associations, young people, adults and older people themselves, the Pontifical Council for the Laity - designated the "focal point" of the coordination of the Holy See's activities for the International Year of Older Persons - hopes that it may help to stimulate reflection and commitment by everyone.

I. MEANING AND VALUE OF OLD AGE

People today live longer and enjoy better health than in the past. They are also able to cultivate interests made possible by higher levels of education. No longer is old age synonymous with dependence on others or a diminished quality of life. But all this seems not enough to dislodge a negative image of old age or encourage a positive acceptance of a period of life in which many of our contemporaries see nothing but an unavoidable and burdensome decline.

The perception of old age as a period of decline, in which human and social inadequacy is taken for granted, is in fact very widespread today. But this is a stereotype. It does not take account of a condition that is in practice far more diversified, because older people are not a homogeneous human group and old age is experienced in very different ways. There are those older people who are capable of grasping the significance that old age has in the context of human existence, and who confront it not only with serenity and dignity, but as a time of life which offers them new opportunities for growth and commitment. But there are others - more numerous in our own day - to whom old age is a traumatic experience, and who react to their own ageing with attitudes ranging from passive resignation to rebellion, rejection and despair. They are persons who become locked into themselves and self-marginalised, thus accelerating the process of their own physical and mental deterioration.

It may thus be affirmed that the aspects of the third and fourth ages are as manifold and varied as older people themselves, and that each of us prepares for old age, and the way we experience it, in the course of our own life. In this sense, old age grows with us. And the quality of our old age will especially depend on our capacity to grasp its meaning and appreciate its value both at the purely human level and at the level of faith. We therefore need to situate old age in the context of a precise providential scheme of God who is love. We need to accept it as a stage in the journey by which Christ leads us to the Father's house (cf. Jn 14:2). Only in the light of the faith, strengthened by the hope which does not deceive (cf. Rom 5:5), shall we be able to accept old age in a truly Christian way both as a gift and a task. That is the secret of the youthfulness of spirit, which we can continue to cultivate in spite of the passing of years. Linda, a woman who lived to the age of 106, left us a magnificent testimony of this. On her 101st birthday, she confided to a friend: "I'm now 101 years old, but I'm strong, you know. Physically I have some disabilities, but spiritually there is nothing I can't do. I don't let physical impediments stand in the way, I pay no attention to them. I don't suffer old age, because I ignore it: it goes ahead on its own, but I pay no heed to it. The only way to live well in old age is to live it in God".

To correct the current, largely negative image of old age is therefore a cultural and educational task which ought to involve all generations. We have a responsibility towards older people today: we need to help them to grasp the sense of their age, to appreciate its resources, and to overcome the temptation to reject it, and so succumb to self-isolation, resignation and a feeling of uselessness and despair. We also have a responsibility towards future generations: that of preparing a human, social and spiritual context in which each person may live this period of life with dignity and fullness.

In his message to the UN's World Assembly on Ageing, Pope John Paul II affirmed: "Life is a gift of God to man who is created out of love in the image and likeness of God. This understanding of the sacred dignity of the human person leads to the appreciation of every stage of life. It is a question of consistency and justice. It is impossible to truly value the life of an older person if the life of a child is not valued from the moment of its conception. No one knows where we might arrive, if life is no longer respected as something inalienable and sacred".[5]

---

5 *Insegnamenti di Giovanni Paolo II*, V, 3 (1982), p. 125.

The multi-generational society we aspire to shall only become an enduring reality if it be based on respect for life in all its phases. The presence of so many older persons in the modern world needs to be recognised as a gift, a new human and spiritual potential for enrichment. It is a sign of the times which, if fully accepted and understood, may help contemporary men and women to rediscover the fundamental meaning of life, which far transcends the purely contingent meanings attributed to it by market forces, by the State and by the prevailing mentality.

The contribution that older people, by their experience, can make to the process of making our society and culture more human is particularly valuable. It needs to be encouraged by fostering what might be termed the charisms proper to old age, namely:

Disinterestedness
The prevailing culture of our time measures the value of our actions according to criteria of efficiency and material success, which ignore the dimension of disinterestedness: of giving something, or giving ourselves, without any thought of a return. Older people, who have time on their hands, may recall the attention of an over-busy society to the need to break down the barriers of an indifference that debases, discourages and stifles altruistic impulses.

Memory
The younger generations are losing a sense of history and consequently the sense of their own identity. A society that minimises the sense of history fails in its responsibility to educate young people. A society that ignores the past more easily runs the risk of repeating its errors. The loss of an historical sense is also attributable to a system of life that has marginalised and isolated older people, and that hampers dialogue between the generations.

Experience
Today we live in a world in which the responses of science and technology seem to have supplanted the value of the experience accumulated by older people in the course of their whole lives. This kind of cultural barrier should not discourage people of the third and fourth ages, since they still have a lot to say to the young generations and to share with them.

Interdependence
No man is an island. But growing individualism and self-seeking are obscuring this truth. Older people, in their search for companionship, challenge a society in which the weaker are often abandoned; they draw attention to the social nature of man and to the need to repair the fabric of interpersonal and social relationships.

A more complete vision of life

Our life is dominated by haste, by agitation, and frequently by neurosis. It is a distracted life, a life in which the fundamental questions about the vocation, dignity and destiny of man are forgotten. The third age is also the age of simplicity and contemplation. The affective, moral and religious values embodied by older people are an indispensable resource for fostering the harmony of society, of the family and of the individual. These values include a sense of responsibility, faith in God, friendship, disinterest in power, prudence, patience, wisdom, and a deep inner conviction of the need to respect the creation and foster peace. Older people understand the superiority of "being" over "having". Human societies would be better if they learnt to benefit from the charisms of old age.

II. THE OLDER PERSON IN THE BIBLE

To grasp in full the sense and value of old age we need to open the Bible. Only the light of the Word of God, in fact, enables us fully to fathom the spiritual, moral and theological dimension of this stage of life. The following biblical passages are presented with the aim of prompting a reconsideration of the meaning of the third and fourth ages. They are accompanied with observations and reflections on the challenges that older people face in contemporary society.

"You will honour the person of the aged" (Lev 19:32)
In the scriptures respect for older people is transformed into a law, a commandment: "You will stand up in the presence of grey hairs ... and fear your God" (Lev 19:32). And again: "Honour your father and your mother" (Deut 5:16). A heartfelt exhortation in favour of parents, especially in their old age, is found in the third chapter of the Book of Sirach (3:16), which concludes with an affirmation of particular gravity: "Whoever deserts a father is no better than a blasphemer, and whoever distresses a mother is accursed of the Lord". We must strive to counter the widespread contemporary tendency to ignore and marginalise older people. We need to "educate" the new generations not to abandon them; young people, adults and older people have a need for each other.

"Our ancestors have told us, of the deeds you did in their days, in days of old, by your hand" (Ps 44:2)

The lives of the patriarchs are particularly eloquent in this regard. When Moses had the experience of the burning bush, God appeared to him as follows: "I am the God of your ancestors, the God of Abraham, the God of Isaac and the God of Jacob" (Ex 3:6). God links his own name with the great patriarchs, who represent the legitimacy and guarantee of the faith of Israel. In the Old Testament, the son, the young person, always encounters - indeed we might almost say "receives" - God from his fathers, from his elders. In the above-cited passage, the recurrent expression "the God of..." denotes that each of the patriarchs had his own personal experience of God. And this experience, which was the legacy of the patriarchs, was also the reason for their youthfulness of spirit and their serenity in the face of death. Paradoxically, it is older people who define the present by transmitting to others what they have received: in a world that extols a condition of eternal youthfulness, shorn of memory or future, this fact cannot but give us pause for thought.

"In old age they will still bear fruit" (Ps 92:14)

The power of God can be revealed in old age, even if it is characterised by physical impediments and difficulties. "God chose those who by human standards are fools to shame the wise; he chose those who by human standards are weak to shame the strong, those who by human standards are common and contemptible - indeed those who count for nothing - to reduce to nothing all those that do count for something, so that no human being might feel boastful before God" (1 Cor 1:27-29). God's plan of salvation is also fulfilled in the fragility of bodies that are weak, barren, impotent and no longer young. It was from Sarah's barren womb and Abraham's centenarian body that the chosen people was born (cf. Rom 4:18-20). And, similarly, it was from Elizabeth's barren womb and the elderly Zechariah that John the Baptist, the precursor of Christ, was born (cf. Lk 1:5-25). Older people, even when their lives take on the semblance of weakness, may, with good reason, consider themselves instruments of the history of salvation: "I shall satisfy him with long life, and grant him to see my salvation" (Ps 91:16), promises the Lord.

"Remember your Creator while you are still young,
before the bad days come, before the years come which,
you will say, give you no pleasure" (Eccles 12:1)
This biblical approach to old age is striking for its disarming objectivity. Moreover, as the Psalmist recalls, our lives are over in a breath, nor is it always gentle and painless: "The span of our life is seventy years, eighty for those who are strong, but their whole extent is anxiety and trouble, they are over in a moment, and we

are gone" (Ps 90:10). The words of Qoheleth in Ecclesiastes - providing a lengthy description of physical decline and death in symbolical images - paint a sombre picture of old age. Holy scripture reminds us here not to harbour any illusions about a period of life that involves hardships, tribulations and sufferings. And it reminds us to look to God throughout our whole life, since he is the goal to which our human pilgrimage is always directed, and especially so in the moment of fear which seizes us when old age is experienced as an ordeal.

*"Abraham breathed his last, dying in a happy ripe age,
old and full of years, and he was gathered to his people"
(Gen 25:8)*
This biblical passage is of particular relevance for our times. The contemporary world has lost sight of the truth about the meaning and value of human life - which God impressed on the conscience of man ever since the creation - and with it the full significance of old age and death. Today, death has lost its sacred character, its sense of fulfilment. It has become taboo. Every effort is made to sweep it under the carpet, to make sure that it does not disturb. Even its setting has changed: it is no longer at home that most people die: older people in particular, increasingly separated from their own human community, ever more frequently die in hospitals or in institutions. Mourning rites and many

forms of piety towards the dead are becoming increasingly rare, especially in the cities. Numbed by the daily images of death presented by the media, people today do everything in their power to avoid coming to terms with a reality which causes them only distress, anxiety and fear. It is inevitable therefore that, as their own death approaches, they are often alone. But the Son of God, who became man, reversed the significance of death: he flung open the doors of hope to those who believe in him: "I am the resurrection. Anyone who believes in me, even though that person dies will live, and whoever lives and believes in me will never die" (Jn 11:25-26). In the light of these words, death - no longer a condemnation, no longer a meaningless epilogue of life signifying nothing - is revealed as a time of hope: the true and certain hope of coming face to face with the Lord.

"Teach us to count up the days that are ours,
and we shall come to the heart of wisdom" (Ps 90:12)
According to the Bible, one of the "charisms of longevity" is wisdom. But wisdom is no automatic prerogative of old age. It is a gift of God, which older people must accept and set as their goal. Only in pursuit of that goal can they attain the wisdom of heart that enables them to "count how few days [they] have", that is, to live the time that Providence grants to each one of us with a sense of responsibility. The essence of this

wisdom is the discovery of the profound meaning of human life and of the transcendent destiny of the person in God. And if this is important for the young, how much more so is it for older people, who are called to direct their lives without losing sight of the "one thing that is necessary" (cf. Lk 10:42).

"In you, Yahweh, I take refuge,
I shall never be put to shame" (Ps 71:1)
This psalm, striking for its beauty, is only one of the many prayers of older people that we find in the Bible and that testify to the religious feelings felt by the soul in the presence of the Lord. Prayer is the principal means for a spiritual understanding of life proper to older people. Prayer is a service. It is a ministry that older people may perform for the good of the whole Church and the world. Even the most infirm and handicapped of them can pray. Prayer is their strength, it is their life. Through prayer they can break down the walls of isolation, emerge from their condition of helplessness, and share in the joys and sorrows of others. Prayer is of central importance. It also touches on the question how an older person can become contemplative in spirit. An older person, confined to bed and reduced to the end of his or her physical strength, can, by praying, become like a monk, a hermit. And through prayer he or she can embrace the whole world. It seems impossible that a person, who has

always lived an active life, can become contemplative. Yet there are moments in life when a frame of mind receptive to contemplation is developed that can benefit the whole of the human community. And prayer is the means *par excellence* to this end, because "there is no renewal, not even social, which does not begin from contemplation. The encounter with God in prayer introduces into the course of history a power ... which touches hearts, leads them to conversion and renewal, and so becomes a powerful historical force transforming social structures".[6]

6 John Paul II, Address to the Italian Church gathered in Palermo for the third Ecclesial Conference, *L'Osservatore Romano*, 24 November 1995, p. 5.

III. OLDER PEOPLE'S PROBLEMS
ARE THE PROBLEMS OF US ALL

Marginalisation

Of the various problems that commonly afflict older people today, one - perhaps more than any other - injures the dignity of the person: marginalisation. The development of this problem, a relatively recent one, has found a fertile breeding ground in a society that cultivates nothing but material success and the glossy image of perennial youth, to the virtual exclusion of those who no longer possess these requisites.

The factors that conspire to consign many older people to the fringes of the human community and civil life are many: evasion of responsibility at the institutional level and consequent social inadequacies; poverty or a drastic reduction of income and of the necessary financial resources to secure a decent standard of living and appropriate levels of care; and the progressive removal of older people from their own family and social environment.

The most painful dimension of this marginalisation, however, is the lack of human relations. Older people suffer not only by being deprived of human contact, but also from abandonment, loneliness and isolation. And as their interpersonal and social contacts are diminished, so their lives are correspondingly impoverished; they are deprived of the intellectual and cultural stimulus and enrichment they need. Older people experience a sense of impotence at being unable to change their own situation, due to their inability to participate in the decision-making processes that concern them both as persons and as citizens. The net result is that they lose any sense of belonging to the community of which they are members.

The problem concerns everyone. It concerns the whole of society. And it is society, at its various institutional levels, that needs to intervene to ensure effective protection, including juridical protection, for that not negligible part of the population that lives in a situation of extreme social, economic and cultural deprivation.

Assistance
Still today - indeed increasingly so - recourse is had to the system of institutional care to assist and treat older people who are infirm, no longer self-sufficient, without any family to look after them, and without adequate financial resources to look after themselves. The confinement of older people in such institutional structures may translate itself into a kind of segregation from society. Some social and welfare policies and the institutions to which they gave rise, however understandable in the light of the different social and

cultural context of the past, have now been rendered obsolete and in conflict with a new human consciousness. A society, aware of its responsibilities towards the older generations who have helped to make it what it is, must strive to create institutions and services adapted to their real needs. Wherever feasible, older people should be given the chance to remain within their own environment by means of such forms of support as home-help, day-care, day-centres, etc.

In this context, a mention of retirement homes is not out of place. By the very fact that they provide accommodation to older persons who have been forced to abandon their own homes, such residential structures are being increasingly urged to respect the autonomy and the personality of each individual, to give each of them the chance to pursue activities linked to his or her own interests, to provide all the forms of care and treatment required by old age, and to give to the accommodation they provide an atmosphere as close to that of the family as possible.

Education and employment
The mentality of our time tends to reinforce the close link between education and professional activity. That is the reason for the lack of educational programmes for older people. In an age in which ongoing training and re-skilling are an essential prerequisite for being able to

keep pace with the rapid progress of technological development and derive material benefits from it, older people - whose level of education is no longer geared to the labour market - are excluded from policies of continuing education. This exclusion ignores their growing needs and aspirations in this field.

Separation from the world of work and from everything related to it occurs today in an over-brusque and inflexible manner. Only rarely does it coincide with the needs, opportunities and preferred choices of the older people concerned. Many older people seek in vain a form of employment; they frequently do so to compensate for inadequate or nonexistent pensions. This need for financial security must be satisfied: older people must be given the chance to do something. They must be enabled to express their own creativity and to develop the spiritual dimension of their lives.

That compulsory retirement can trigger off a process of premature ageing now seems demonstrated. Conversely, the pursuit of some form of employment beyond retirement age would have a beneficial effect on the quality of life of older people. The spare time that they have on their hands is therefore the first resource that needs to be addressed. An active role needs to be restored to them. Their access to the new technologies, and employment in socially useful forms of work, need to be promoted; and opportunities of engaging in forms of volunteer work and services of benefit to the community, opened up to them.

Participation
It is an established fact that older people, if they are given the opportunity, do participate actively in the life of the community, both at the civil and at the cultural and associational levels. This is confirmed by the numerous positions of responsibility held by older persons, for example in the field of the volunteer services, and by their far from negligible political influence. Steps must be taken to correct the lack of representation of older people, and to remove the prejudices and misconceptions that have damaged their image in our time.

Older people must be enabled to influence the policies that concern their life, but also those that concern society in general. They must be helped to do so through specific organisations, and through appropriate forms of political and trade union representation. The creation of associations for older people must therefore be encouraged, and those already existing be supported. Such associations, as John Paul II has stressed, "must be recognised by the authorities in society as a legitimate expression of the voice of older people, and especially of those older people who are most dispossessed".[7]

To stem the culture of indifference, rampant individualism, competitiveness and utilitarianism which are now threatening all areas of society, and to remove any form of segregation between the generations, a new mentality, a new attitude, a new mode of being, a new culture need to be developed. A form of prosperity and of social justice needs to be pursued that is compatible with the objective of defending the centrality of the human person and his dignity.

7 *Insegnamenti di Giovanni Paolo II*, V, 3 (1982), p. 130.

IV. THE CHURCH AND OLDER PEOPLE

"The life of older people ... helps to cast light on the scale of human values; to reveal the continuity of the generations and wonderfully to demonstrate the interdependence of the people of God".[8] It is notably in the Church that this interdependence is expressed: it is there that the various generations are called to share in the plan of God's love by reciprocally exchanging the gifts with which each person is enriched by grace of the Holy Spirit. To this exchange of gifts older people bring religious and moral values that represent a rich spiritual endowment for the life of Christian communities, families and the world.

Religious practice occupies a key place in the life of older persons. The third age seems particularly conducive to transcendental values. Confirmation of this is given, among other things, by the frequent and numerous participation of older people in liturgical celebrations, by the unexpected return of many of them to the Church after long years of absence, and by the important role played by prayer in their lives. Prayer represents in fact an inestimable contribution to the spiritual resources of devotion and sacrifice, from which the Church copiously draws and which need to be fostered both within Christian communities and within families.

8 *Insegnamenti di Giovanni Paolo II*, III, 2 (1980), p. 539.

Often lived in a simple way, but not for that reason any less profound, the religious faith of older people of both sexes is highly diversified; this is also determined by the relative strength of their faith in their earlier life.

At times, it is distinguished by a kind of fatalism: in such cases, suffering, disabilities, illnesses, the losses inseparable from this phase of life, are regarded, if not as divine punishments, at least as signs of a God who is no longer benevolent. The ecclesial community has the responsibility to purify this fatalism by helping to develop the religious faith of older people and by restoring a horizon of hope to it.

In this task, catechesis has a role of primary importance to play. It is the job of catechesis to purge faith of fear, to overcome the image of a wrathful God, and to lead the older person to discover the God of love. Familiarity with holy scripture, a deeper knowledge of the content of our faith, and meditation on the death and resurrection of Christ will help older people to overcome a punitive conception of God, which bears no relation to his love as a Father. By participating in the liturgical and sacramental prayer of the Christian community and by sharing its life, older people will increasingly learn to understand that the Lord is not uncaring, not indifferent to human sorrow or to the personal difficulties they encounter in the course of their lives.

It is the duty of the Church to announce to older people the good news of Jesus, who is revealed to them just as he was revealed to Simeon and Anna. Jesus comforts them with his presence. He causes their hearts to rejoice at the fulfilment of hopes and promises that they had kept alive in their hearts (cf. Lk 2:25-38).

It is the duty of the Church to give older people the chance to encounter Christ. She must help them to rediscover the significance of their baptism, by means of which they were buried together with Christ and joined him in death, "so that as Christ was raised from the dead by the Father's glorious power, [they] too should begin living a new life" (Rom 6:4) and find in him the meaning of their present and future life. For hope is rooted in faith in this presence of the Spirit of God, "the Spirit of him who raised Jesus from the dead" and who will also give life to our own mortal bodies (cf. Rom 8:11). Consciousness of rebirth in baptism enables older people to preserve in their hearts a childlike awe before the mystery of the love of God revealed in the creation and redemption.

It is the duty of the Church to instil older people with a deep awareness of the task they too have of transmitting the gospel of Christ to the world, and revealing to everyone the mystery of his abiding presence in history. It is also her duty to make them aware of their responsibility as privileged witnesses, who can testify - both before human society and before the Christian community - to God's fidelity: he always keeps the promises he has made to man.

The pastoral task of evangelising or re-evangelising older members of the community must aim at fostering the spirituality that is peculiar to this age of life: i.e. a spirituality based on the continual rebirth that Jesus himself recommended to the elderly Nicodemus. Jesus urged Nicodemus not to let old age stand in the way of rebirth. To be reborn to a life that is ever new and full of hope, we don't need to go back to our mother's womb: we need to be "born from above", by opening ourselves up to the gift of the Spirit; for "what is born of human nature is human; what is born of the Spirit is spirit" (Jn 3:6).

Christ's call to holiness is addressed to all his disciples, in every phase of human life: "You must therefore set no bounds to your love, just as your heavenly Father sets none to his" (Mt 5:48). In spite of the passing of years, which risks dampening enthusiasm and draining away energy, older people must therefore feel themselves more than ever called to persevere in the search for Christian holiness: Christians must never let apathy or tiredness impede their spiritual journey.

This pastoral task involves the need to train priests, assistants and volunteers - young people, adults, older people themselves - for service to older people; pastoral workers who are imbued with humanity and spirituality, and who have the ability to enter into rapport with people in the third and fourth ages, and to respond to their often very individualised human, social, cultural and spiritual needs.

The needs of older people must also be addressed by the various branches of specialised pastoral care. These include the family apostolate, which cannot ignore the bonds between older people and their family, not only at the level of social services, but also at that of religious life; the various forms of social ministry; and the apostolate of health-care workers.

The contribution that older people themselves can make is also indispensable to this pastoral work. From their rich endowment of faith and of experience they can draw things old and new to the advantage not only of themselves, but also of the whole community. Far from being the passive recipients of the Church's pastoral care, older people are irreplaceable apostles, especially among their own age group, because no one is more familiar than they with the problems and the feelings of this phase of life. Particular importance is being given today, moreover, to the apostolate of older people among people of their own age group in the form of witness of life. As Paul VI wrote in *Evangelii Nuntiandi*, modern man "listens more willingly to witness than to teachers, and if he does listen to teachers, it is because they are witnesses" (n. 41). So it is not of secondary importance to be able to show, in concrete terms, that this season of life, when lived in a Christian way, has a value of its own, enriched by the profound significance that it acquires through the whole course of human existence. No less important is the direct preaching of the Word of God by one older person to another, or to the up-and-coming generations of children and grandchildren.

By word and by prayer, and also by the renunciations and sufferings that advanced age brings with it, older people have always been eloquent witnesses and apostles of the faith in Christian communities and in families - sometimes in conditions of persecution, as was the case, for example, under the atheist totalitarian regimes of the Communist bloc in the twentieth century. Who has not heard of the Russian *"babushkas"*, who kept alive the faith during the long decades when any expression of religious faith was equivalent to a criminal activity, and who transmitted it to their grandchildren? It was thanks to their courage and steadfastness that faith was not completely extinguished in the former Communist countries and that a basis now exists - albeit a precarious one - for the new evangelisation to build on. The International Year of Older Persons offers a valuable occasion to remember these extraordinary older people - both men and women - and their silent and heroic witness. Not only the Church, but human civilisation is greatly indebted to them.

An important role in promoting the active participation of older people in the work of evangelisation is now played by the Church-based associations and the ecclesial movements, "one of the gifts of the Spirit [to the Church] of our time".[9] Many older people have already found an extremely fertile field for their formation, commitment and apostolate in the various associations present in our parishes. They have become real protagonists within the Christian community. Nor is there any lack of other groups, communities and movements working more specifically in the world of the third age. Thanks to their charisms, all these associations create an environment in which communion can thrive between the various generations and a spiritual climate that helps older people to maintain their spiritual vitality and youthfulness.

9 John Paul II, Homily during the Vigil of Pentecost, *L'Osservatore Romano*, 27-28 May 1996, p. 7.

V. GUIDELINES FOR THE PASTORAL CARE OF OLDER PEOPLE

Sharing "the joy and hope, the grief and anguish of the men of our time",[10] the Church strives with maternal solicitude to support older people through forms of assistance and charitable activities. She also urges older people to continue their own evangelising mission, which it is not only possible and necessary, but which is in some sense a specific and original task of this age of life.

In the post-synodal apostolic exhortation *Christifideles Laici* on the vocation and mission of the laity, John Paul II, addressing older people, writes: "The expected retirement of persons from various professions and the workplace provides older people with a new opportunity in the apostolate. Involved in the task is their determination to overcome the temptation of taking refuge in a nostalgia in a never-to-return past or fleeing from present responsibility because of difficulties encountered in a world of one novelty after another. They must always have a clear knowledge that one's role in the Church and society does not stop at a certain age at all, but at such times knows only new ways of application. ... Arriving at an older age is to be

10 Pastoral constitution on the Church in the modern world *Gaudium et Spes*, n. 1.

considered a privilege: not simply because not everyone has the good fortune to reach this stage in life, but also, and above all, because this period provides real possibilities for better evaluating the past, for knowing and living more deeply the paschal mystery, for becoming an example in the Church for the whole people of God" (n. 48).

The ecclesial community, for its part, is called to respond to the greater participation which older people would like to have in the Church, by turning to account the "gift" they represent as witnesses of the tradition of faith (cf. Ps 44:2; Ex 12:26-27), teachers of the wisdom of life (cf. Sir 6:34; 8:11-12) and workers of charity. It must therefore reexamine its apostolate on behalf of older people, and open it up to their participation and collaboration.

Of the various areas that best lend themselves to the witness of older people in the Church the following should not be forgotten:

Charitable activities
A large proportion of older people have enough physical, mental and spiritual energies to devote their own time and talents in a generous way to the various activities and programmes of the volunteer services.

Apostolate

Older people can make a major contribution to the preaching of the gospel as catechists and witnesses to Christian life.

Liturgy

Many older people already contribute effectively to the service of places of worship. If suitably trained, they could, in larger numbers, play the role of permanent deacons, and fulfil the ministry of lector and altar server. They could also be used in the extraordinary ministry of the Eucharist, and exercise the role of animators of the liturgy. They could also help promote forms of Eucharistic devotion and other forms of devotion, especially to Mary and to the saints.

Ecclesial associations and movements

Especially in the aftermath of the Second Vatican Council older people began to show a more marked interest in the community dimension of their faith. The growth of many ecclesial associations and communities - which represent a great enrichment for the Church - is also due to a form of participation that integrates the various generations, and manifests the richness and fruitfulness of the different charisms of the Spirit.

The family
Older people represent the "historical memory" of the younger generations. They are the bearers of fundamental human values. Where this memory is lacking, people are rootless; they also lack any capacity to project themselves with hope towards a future that transcends the limits of the present. The family - and hence society as a whole - will benefit greatly from a re-evaluation of the educational role of older people.

Contemplation and prayer
Older people should be encouraged to consecrate the years that remain hidden in the mind of God to a new mission illuminated by the Holy Spirit. In this way they may give rise to a stage of human life which, in the light of the paschal mystery of the Lord, is revealed as the richest and most promising of all. In this regard, John Paul II, addressing the participants at the International Forum on Ageing, said: "Older people, with the wisdom and experience which are the fruit of a lifetime, have entered upon a time of extraordinary grace which opens to them new opportunities for prayer and union with God. Called to serve others and to offer their lives to the Lord and Giver of Life, new spiritual powers are given to them".[11]

11 *Insegnamenti di Giovanni Paolo II*, III, 2 (1980), p. 538.

Trials, illnesses and suffering
These experiences represent the "fulfilment", in body and heart, of the passion of Christ for the Church and for the world (cf. Col 1:24). It is important that older people - and not only they - be helped to accept these crosses in a spirit of humble submission to the will of God, in imitation of the Lord. But this will only be possible in proportion as they feel loved and esteemed. Devotion to the weak, to the suffering, to the disabled is a duty of the Church and is proof of her maternal care. A whole series of services and forms of pastoral care should therefore be provided to ensure that older people do not feel useless and a burden, and to help them to accept their suffering as a means of encountering the mystery of God and of man.

Commitment to a "culture of life"
Illness and suffering are privileged means for reminding us of the inalienable principle of the sacredness and inviolability of life. The mission of Jesus itself, with its many cases of healing the sick and disabled, shows how much God has at heart not only the spiritual but also the bodily life of man (cf. Lk 4:18). Man cannot arbitrarily choose to live or die, or decide on the life or death of others: that is a choice which only he in whom "we live, and move and exist" (Acts 17:28; cf. Dt 32:39) can make. The exclusion of, or blindness to,

the transcendental dimension, typical of our own times, is increasingly promoting a tendency to appreciate life only in so far as it produces pleasure and wellbeing, and to regard suffering as an intolerable burden which needs to be eliminated at all costs. Death, regarded as "absurd" if it curtails a life still full of promising and exciting potential, is regarded as a "liberation", to be claimed as a right, if it terminates a life seen as meaningless because overwhelmed by suffering. It is this attitude that forms the cultural context of euthanasia, which the Church condemns as "a grave violation of the law of God, since it is the deliberate and morally unacceptable killing of a human person".[12]

In view of the great diversity in the situations and conditions of the life of older people, the Church's pastoral ministry to those in the third and fourth ages ought to involve the implementation of a series of measures aimed at achieving the following objectives:

Consciousness raising
The Church should heighten awareness of the needs of older people, not least that of being able to contribute to the life of the community by performing activities appropriate to their condition. This awareness will

12 John Paul II, Encyclical letter *Evangelium Vitae*, n. 65.

permit the formulation of qualified forms of intervention. It will also sensitise and involve both the ecclesial and civil communities; and focus attention on those options that are revealed as evangelically and culturally more valid, also with a view to a renewal of the Church's charitable works and forms of assistance.

Countering attitudes of withdrawal
Older people must be helped to overcome the indifference and mistrust that hamper their active participation and solidarity.

Promoting integration
Older people must be integrated, without any form of discrimination, into the Christian community. All the baptised, in every moment of life, must be able to renew the richness of grace of their own baptism and fully experience it in their lives. No one should be deprived of the grace of God, the preaching of the Word, the consolation of prayer or the witness of charity.

Developing the service of older people in the community
The life of the Christian community must be organised in such a way as to encourage the participation of older persons and to foster the capacities of each. To this end, the dioceses should set up their own diocesan offices for the ministry to older people; and parishes should be encouraged to develop spiritual, community and

recreational activities for this age group. The service of older people should also be promoted within diocesan and parish councils and within councils for economic affairs.

Participation in the sacramental life of the Church
Older people must be helped to participate in the celebration of the Eucharist, in the sacrament of reconciliation and in pilgrimages, retreats and spiritual exercises. Steps should also be taken to ensure that their involvement in such events be not hindered by physical or architectural barriers, or by the lack of specialised personnel to accompany and assist them.

Spiritual care
The care and assistance of older people who are infirm or disabled, or no longer in full possession of their physical or mental faculties, should also involve spiritual care; through prayer and communion in the faith, it should testify to the inalienable value of life, even when it is reduced to a terminal condition.

Sacrament of the sick and dying
The administration of the sacrament of the anointing of the sick and of viaticum must be fostered in a special way, and preceded by appropriate catechesis. Where circumstances permit, it is desirable that priests incorporate the sacrament of anointing the sick in

community celebrations both in the parishes and in the places of residence in which older people live.

Comforting the terminally ill
Efforts should be made to resist the tendency to abandon the dying and leave them without religious assistance and human comfort. This task is not only incumbent on chaplains, whose role is fundamental, but also on the families and communities to which older people belong.

Caring for those of other faiths
Particular attention should be devoted, in a spirit of charity and dialogue, to the elderly of other religious confessions in order to help them live their faith; nor should Christians be shy of witnessing to their own faith, in a spirit of brotherhood and solidarity, to older people who are nonbelievers.

A rightful place in society and in the family
Older people have a right to a place in society and even more so to an honoured place within the family. The family is called to be a communion of persons. It needs to be reminded of its special mission to foster, manifest and communicate love, and its duty to provide assistance to its weaker members, not least the elderly, and surround them with affection. The need for the

family to be able to benefit from adequate means of material support should also be emphasised: economic assistance, welfare and health services, and appropriate housing, pension and social security policies should be available to the needs of the family.

Caring for older people living in public or private residential structures
The uprooting of older people from their natural families would be less traumatic if the community were to maintain links with them. The parish community, "family of families", must turn itself into a *"diaconia"* at the service of older people and their problems. It must also seek to cooperate with the authorities responsible for running such residential homes with a view to finding appropriate ways to ensure the involvement of the volunteer services, the provision of cultural activities and religious service. The latter must ensure that older people are able to be nourished by the Eucharist, and that Holy Communion assumes its significance as participation in the celebration of the Lord's Day. The Eucharist must be made present to older people as a sign of the fatherhood of God and of the fruitfulness of life and suffering which risk sinking into grief and even despair, if they are not illuminated by the comfort of the Lord.

Caring for elderly priests

It should never be forgotten that the ranks of older people also include priests, ministers of the Church and pastors of Christian communities. The diocesan Church must assume responsibility for looking after these elderly priests, and provide them with adequate residential structures and other forms of support. Parish communities too are called to make their contribution; they should take steps to ensure that elderly priests who retire from their active ministry as a result of old age or poor health find appropriate accommodation. The same goes for religious communities and their superiors, who should devote particular care to their older brothers and sisters.

Inter-generational solidarity

The young members of groups, associations and movements present in the parishes must be educated to show solidarity towards the elder members of the community. Such inter-generational solidarity is also expressed in the companionship that the young are able to offer to the old. Young people who have opportunities for involvement with older people will appreciate the value of a formative experience by which they gain in maturity and are helped to develop an awareness of others that remains with them for the whole of their life. In a society in which selfishness, materialism, consumerism are rife and in which the means of communication serve little to alleviate the growing loneliness of man, such values as selflessness, dedication, friendship, acceptance and respect represent a challenge to those, not least the young, who are striving for the birth of a new humanity.

The pastoral ministry to older people as a whole, and those involved in it, will derive particular illumination and guidance from constant reference to the conciliar decree on the apostolate of lay people *Apostolicam Actuositatem*, and to the documents issued by the magisterium of the Church in recent years, especially the post-synodal apostolic exhortation *Christifideles Laici*, the apostolic letter *Salvifici Doloris* and the apostolic exhortation *Familiaris Consortio*.

CONCLUSIONS

Our brief exploration of the world of the third and fourth ages has thrown light on many problems associated with old age, which demand specific responses from civil society and special attention from the ecclesial community. But it has also revealed the richness in humanity and wisdom of older people, who still have a great deal to offer to the Church and to society.

To accompany older people, to approach them and enter into relation with them, is the duty of us all. The time has come to begin working towards an effective change in attitude towards older people and to restore to them their rightful place in the human community.

Society and its institutions are called to give older people scope for personal development and participation, and provide them with forms of social assistance and health-care consonant with their needs and responding to the need of the human person to live with dignity, in justice and freedom. To this end, alongside the commitment of the State aimed at promoting and safeguarding the common good, the involvement of the volunteer services and the contribution of initiatives inspired by Christian charity need to be supported and fostered, in full respect for the principle of subsidiarity.

The Christian community must strive to help older persons to live their own life in the light of the faith and to rediscover in it the value of the resources that they are still able, and still have a responsibility, to place at the service of others. Older people must become increasingly conscious that they have a future before them that they themselves must shape. They must be made aware that their missionary task is not exhausted. They still have a responsibility to testify to children, young people, adults and those in their own age group that there is no meaning nor joy outside the bond with Christ, neither in their own personal lives not in their relations with others.

"The harvest is rich" (Mt 9:37). These words of the Lord are particularly applicable to the field of the pastoral care of older people. It is a field so extensive as to require the generous work and passionate commitment of countless apostles, workers and witnesses who can testify convincingly to the fullness of life that can characterise this season of life if it be founded on the "rock" that is Christ (cf. Mt 7:24-27).

An extraordinary example of this truth is given to us by Pope John Paul II: in this too he is a great witness to men and women in our time. The Pope lives his old age with the greatest naturalism. Far from concealing it (who has not seen him joke with his walking stick?), he places it before everyone's eyes. With extreme simplicity, he says of himself: "I'm an elderly priest". He lives his old age in faith, in the service of the mission entrusted to him by Christ. He does not let himself be conditioned by his age. His seventy-eight years have not deprived him of his youthfulness of spirit. Nor has his undeniable physical fragility dampened the enthusiasm with which he dedicates himself to his mission as successor of Peter. He tirelessly continues his apostolic journeys across the continents. And it is striking to note that his words acquire ever greater force: now more than ever they reach people's hearts.

Service to older people, especially if accompanied by a pastoral care alert to the diversity of needs and charisms, open to everyone's participation, and aimed at exploiting everyone's capacities, represents an enrichment for the whole Church. It is therefore desirable that as many as possible embrace this service, and that they grasp its profound significance as a process of conversion of heart and reciprocal giving between the generations.

The year 1999, dedicated to older people by the United Nations, is also the year dedicated to God the Father as part of the preparation for the Great Jubilee of the year 2000: a providential coincidence, which can provide the younger generations with an occasion to reflect on and reestablish their relations with the older generations. It can also provide those who are no longer young with an occasion to reexamine their own existence and to place it in the joyful perspective of bearing witness that "the whole of the Christian life is like a great pilgrimage to the house of the Father, whose unconditional love for every human creature we discover anew each day".[13]

In the year 2000, the jubilee year which introduces the people of God to the third millennium of the Christian era, a special day, 17 September, will be dedicated to older people. We are confident that they will not overlook this important date. We are also confident that the prospect of the Great Jubilee will inspire initiatives - at the local, diocesan, national and international level - that will permit older people to express ever more strongly and in ever growing numbers their capacity to participate, to give hope and to receive hope. For only with older people, and thanks to them, shall the praises of the Lord be joyfully sung for ever and ever (cf. Ps 79:13).

From the Vatican, 1 October 1998.

JAMES FRANCIS Card. STAFFORD
President

+ STANISLAW RYLKO
STANISLAW RYLKO
Secretary

13 John Paul II, Apostolic letter *Tertio Millennio Adveniente*, n. 49.